noggins and necks

Let the wind blow and the snowflakes fall—you'll have five cozy reasons to smile through it all! That's because Bonnie Barker's stunning hat-and-scarf sets can be crocheted in a weekend or less. Bonnie says, "My best friend's mom taught me to read fisherman crochet patterns from a Leisure Arts book. I based some of these new designs on that richly textured style, while all five sets are closely worked for warmth. They finish quickly and make beautiful gifts."

LEISURE ARTS, INC.
Little Rock, Arkansas

W9-BWU-971

basket weave
HAT & SCARF SET

 **EASY**

Finished Sizes
Scarf: 6¼"w x 60"l (16 cm x 152.5 cm)
Hat: Fits 21" (53.5 cm) head circumference

MATERIALS
Medium Weight Yarn **(4)**
[3 ounces, 197 yards
(85 grams, 180 meters) per skein]:
   4 skeins
Crochet hook, size J (6 mm) **or** size needed
   for gauge

GAUGE: In pattern,
            14 sts and 8 rows = 4" (10 cm)

Gauge Swatch: 6¼"w x 4"h (16 cm x 10 cm)
Work same as Scarf for 8 rows.

STITCH GUIDE
FRONT POST DOUBLE CROCHET
   (abbreviated FPdc)
YO, insert hook from **front** to **back** around
post of st indicated *(Fig. 3, page 19)*, YO and
pull up a loop (3 loops on hook), (YO and
draw through 2 loops on hook) twice.
BACK POST DOUBLE CROCHET
   (abbreviated BPdc)
YO, insert hook from **back** to **front** around
post of st indicated *(Fig. 3, page 19)*, YO and
pull up a loop (3 loops on hook), (YO and
draw through 2 loops on hook) twice.

SCARF
Ch 24.

Row 1: Dc in fourth ch from hook **(3 skipped
chs count as first dc)** and in each ch across:
22 dc.

Row 2: Ch 2 **(counts as first hdc, now and
throughout)**, turn; work FPdc around each of
next 4 dc, ★ work BPdc around each of next
4 dc, work FPdc around each of next 4 dc;
repeat from ★ once **more**, hdc in last dc.

Row 3: Ch 2, turn; work BPdc around each of
next 4 sts, ★ work FPdc around each of next
4 sts, work BPdc around each of next 4 sts;
repeat from ★ once **more**, hdc in last hdc.

Rows 4 and 5: Ch 2, turn; work FPdc around
each of next 4 sts, ★ work BPdc around each of
next 4 sts, work FPdc around each of next 4 sts;
repeat from ★ once **more**, hdc in last hdc.

Instructions continued on page 4.

Row 6: Ch 2, turn; work BPdc around each of next 4 sts, ★ work FPdc around each of next 4 sts, work BPdc around each of next 4 sts; repeat from ★ once **more**, hdc in last hdc.

Row 7: Ch 2, turn; work FPdc around each of next 4 sts, ★ work BPdc around each of next 4 sts, work FPdc around each of next 4 sts; repeat from ★ once **more**, hdc in last hdc.

Rows 8 and 9: Ch 2, turn; work BPdc around each of next 4 sts, ★ work FPdc around each of next 4 sts, work BPdc around each of next 4 sts; repeat from ★ once **more**, hdc in last hdc.

Row 10: Ch 2, turn; work FPdc around each of next 4 sts, ★ work BPdc around each of next 4 sts, work FPdc around each of next 4 sts; repeat from ★ once **more**, hdc in last hdc.

Repeat Rows 3-10 for pattern until Scarf measures approximately 60" (152.5 cm) **or** desired length, ending by working Row 4 or Row 8.

Finish off.

HAT

Ch 4; join with slip st to form a ring.

Rnd 1 (Right side)**:** Ch 1, 14 sc in ring; join with slip st to first sc.

Rnd 2: Ch 2, 2 dc in first sc and in each sc around; join with slip st to top of beginning ch-2: 28 dc.

Rnd 3: Ch 2, 2 dc in first dc and in each dc around; join with slip st to top of beginning ch-2: 56 dc.

Rnd 4: Ch 2, work FPdc around each of first 4 dc, work BPdc around each of next 4 dc, ★ work FPdc around each of next 4 dc, work BPdc around each of next 4 dc; repeat from ★ around; join with slip st to top of beginning ch-2.

Rnds 5 and 6: Ch 2, work FPdc around each of first 4 FPdc, work BPdc around each of next 4 BPdc, ★ work FPdc around each of next 4 FPdc, work BPdc around each of next 4 BPdc; repeat from ★ around; join with slip st to top of beginning ch-2.

Rnd 7: Ch 2, work BPdc around each of first 4 FPdc, work FPdc around each of next 4 BPdc, ★ work BPdc around each of next 4 FPdc, work FPdc around each of next 4 BPdc; repeat from ★ around; join with slip st to top of beginning ch-2.

Rnds 8-10: Ch 2, work BPdc around each of first 4 BPdc, work FPdc around each of next 4 FPdc, ★ work BPdc around each of next 4 BPdc, work FPdc around each of next 4 FPdc; repeat from ★ around; join with slip st to top of beginning ch-2.

Rnd 11: Ch 2, work FPdc around each of first 4 BPdc, work BPdc around each of next 4 FPdc, ★ work FPdc around each of next 4 BPdc, work BPdc around each of next 4 FPdc; repeat from ★ around; join with slip st to top of beginning ch-2.

Rnds 12-14: Ch 2, work FPdc around each of first 4 FPdc, work BPdc around each of next 4 BPdc, ★ work FPdc around each of next 4 FPdc, work BPdc around each of next 4 BPdc; repeat from ★ around; join with slip st to top of beginning ch-2.

Rnds 15-25: Repeat Rnds 7-14 once, then repeat Rnds 7-9 once **more**.

Finish off.

Fold edge up for brim.

woven stitch
HAT & SCARF SET

Shown on page 7.

◐◼◻◻ **EASY**

Finished Sizes
Scarf: 6³/₄"w x 62"l (17 cm x 157.5 cm)
Hat: Fits 21" (53.5 cm) head circumference

MATERIALS
Medium Weight Yarn **MEDIUM ④**
[7 ounces, 382 yards
(197 grams, 350 meters) per skein]:
  2 skeins
Crochet hook, size J (6 mm) **or** size needed
  for gauge
Yarn needle

GAUGE: 12 sc and 12 rows = 4" (10 cm)

Gauge Swatch: 4" (10 cm) square
Ch 13.
Row 1: Sc in second ch from hook and in each
ch across: 12 sc.
Rows 2-12: Ch 1, turn; sc in each sc across.
Finish off.

STITCH GUIDE
TREBLE CROCHET *(abbreviated tr)*
YO twice, insert hook in st indicated,
YO and pull up a loop (4 loops on hook),
(YO and draw through 2 loops on hook)
3 times.
WOVEN ST (uses one st or sp)
YO, insert hook in st or sp indicated, YO
and pull loop through st or sp **and** through
one loop on hook, YO and draw through
remaining 2 loops on hook, YO, insert hook
in **same** st or sp, YO and pull loop through
st or sp **and** through both loops on hook.
DECREASE
Pull up a loop in each of next 2 sc, YO and
draw through all 3 loops on hook (**counts as
one sc**).

SCARF
Ch 187.

Row 1 (Right side)**:** Sc in second ch from hook
and in each ch across: 186 sc.

Note: Loop a short piece of yarn around any
stitch to mark Row 1 as **right** side.

Row 2: Ch 2, turn; skip first sc, work Woven
st in next sc, (skip next sc, work Woven st in
next sc) across: 93 Woven sts.

Rows 3-5: Ch 2, turn; ★ skip next Woven st,
work Woven st in sp **before** next Woven st
(Fig. 4, page 19); repeat from ★ across to last
Woven st, skip last Woven st, work Woven st in
sp **before** beginning ch-2.

Row 6: Ch 1, turn; (skip next Woven st, 2 sc
in sp **before** next Woven st) across to last
Woven st, skip last Woven st, 2 sc in sp **before**
beginning ch-2: 186 sc.

Instructions continued on page 6.

Row 7: Ch 1, turn; slip st in Front Loop Only of each sc across *(Fig. 2, page 18)*.

Row 8: Ch 1, turn; working in free loops of sc one row **below** *(Fig. 1a, page 18)*, sc in each sc across.

Row 9: Ch 3 **(counts as first dc, now and throughout)**, turn; working in both loops, skip next 3 sc, tr in next sc, working **behind** tr just made, dc in each skipped sc, ★ skip next 3 sc from last tr made, tr in next sc, working **behind** tr just made, dc in each skipped sc; repeat from ★ across to last sc, dc in last sc: 140 dc and 46 tr.

Row 10: Ch 3, turn; skip next 3 dc, tr in next tr, working in **front** of tr just made, dc in each skipped dc, ★ skip next 3 dc from last tr made, tr in next tr, working in **front** of tr just made, dc in each skipped dc; repeat from ★ across to last dc, dc in last dc.

Rows 11 and 12: Ch 1, turn; sc in each st across: 186 sc.

Row 13: Ch 1, turn; slip st in Front Loop Only of each sc across.

Row 14: Ch 1, turn; working in free loops of sc one row **below**, sc in each sc across.

Rows 15-19: Working in both loops, repeat Rows 2-6.

Edging Rnd: Ch 1, turn; slip st in each sc across, ch 1; work 16 sc evenly spaced across end of rows, ch 1; working in free loops of beginning ch *(Fig. 1b, page 18)*, slip st in each ch across, ch 1; work 16 sc evenly spaced across end of rows, ch 1; join with slip st to first slip st, finish off.

HAT
BODY
Ch 23.

Row 1 (Right side)**:** Sc in second ch from hook and in each ch across: 22 sc.

Note: Mark Row 1 as **right** side.

Row 2: Ch 1, turn; sc in each sc across.

Row 3: Ch 1, turn; slip st in Front Loop Only of each sc across.

Row 4: Ch 1, turn; working in free loops of sc one row **below**, sc in each sc across.

Row 5: Ch 3, turn; working in both loops, skip next 3 sc, tr in next sc, working **behind** tr just made, dc in each skipped sc, ★ skip next 3 sc from last tr made, tr in next sc, working **behind** tr just made, dc in each skipped sc; repeat from ★ across to last sc, dc in last sc: 17 dc and 5 tr.

Row 6: Ch 3, turn; skip next tr and next 3 dc, tr in next tr, working in **front** of tr just made, dc in each skipped dc, ★ skip next 3 dc from last tr made, tr in next tr, working in **front** of tr just made, dc in each skipped dc; repeat from ★ across to last dc, dc in last dc.

Rows 7 and 8: Ch 1, turn; sc in each st across: 22 sc.

Row 9: Ch 1, turn; slip st in Front Loop Only of each sc across.

Row 10: Ch 1, turn; working in free loops of of sc one row **below**, sc in each sc across.

Row 11: Ch 2, turn; skip first sc, work Woven st in next sc, (skip next sc, work Woven st in next sc) across: 11 Woven sts.

Rows 12-15: Ch 2, turn; (skip next Woven st, work Woven st in sp **before** next Woven st) across to last Woven st, skip last Woven st, work Woven st in ch-2 sp.

Row 16: Ch 1, turn; (skip next Woven st, 2 sc in sp **before** next Woven st) across to last Woven st, skip last Woven st, 2 sc in ch-2 sp: 22 sc.

Rows 17-58: Repeat Rows 3-16, 3 times.

Joining Row: Ch 1, turn; with **right** side together, matching free loops of beginning ch with sc on Row 58, slip st in each st across working through **both** thicknesses; do **not** finish off.

CROWN

Rnd 1: Ch 1, turn; with **right** side facing and working in end of rows on Body, work 54 sc evenly spaced around; join with slip st to first sc.

Rnd 2: Ch 1, do **not** turn; beginning in same st as joining, decrease around; join with slip st to first sc: 27 sc.

Rnd 3: Ch 1, sc in same st, decrease, (sc in next sc, decrease) around; join with slip st to first sc: 18 sc.

Rnd 4: Ch 1, beginning in same st, decrease around; join with slip st to first sc: 9 sc.

Rnd 5: Ch 1, sc in same st, decrease around; join with slip st to first sc, finish off leaving a long end for sewing: 5 sc.

Thread yarn needle with long end and weave through sts on Rnd 5; pull **tightly** to close and secure end.

BRIM

Foundation Rnd: With **right** side facing, using smaller size hook, and working in end of rows on Body, join yarn with slip st in any row; ch 1, work 54 sc evenly spaced around; join with slip st to first sc.

Row 1: Ch 10, sc in second ch from hook and in each ch across; slip st in next 2 sc on Foundation Rnd: 9 sc and 2 slip sts.

Row 2: Ch 1, turn; skip first 2 slip sts, sc in Back Loop Only of each sc across *(Fig. 2, page 18)*: 9 sc.

Row 3: Ch 1, turn; sc in Back Loop Only of each sc across; slip st in both loops of next 2 sc on Foundation Rnd: 9 sc and 2 slip sts.

Rows 4-52: Repeat Rows 2 and 3, 24 times; then repeat Row 2 once **more**.

Row 53: Ch 1, turn; sc in Back Loop Only of each sc across; slip st in **both** loops of next 2 sc on Foundation Rnd, slip st in same sc on Foundation Rnd (last slip st is worked in same st as Foundation Rnd joining).

Joining Row: Ch 1, turn; matching sc on Row 53 with free loops of beginning ch-10 and working through **both** thicknesses, slip st in Back Loop Only of sc **and** in free loop of beginning ch across; finish off.

Fold edge up for Brim.

two stitch
HAT & SCARF SET

 **EASY**

Finished Sizes
Scarf: 6½"w x 60"l (16.5 cm x 152.5 cm)
Hat: Fits 21" (53.5 cm) head circumference

MATERIALS
Medium Weight Yarn
[6 ounces, 312 yards
(170 grams, 285 meters) per skein]:
   2 skeins
Crochet hook, size J (6 mm) **or** size needed
   for gauge

GAUGE: In pattern,
        11 sts and 10 rows = 4" (10 cm)

Gauge Swatch: 6½"w x 4"h (16.5 cm x 10 cm)
Work same as Scarf through Row 10.

SCARF
Ch 19.

Row 1: Sc in second ch from hook, dc in next ch, (sc in next ch, dc in next ch) across: 18 sts.

Row 2: Ch 1, turn; sc in first dc, dc in next sc, (sc in next dc, dc in next sc) across.

Repeat Row 2 for pattern until Scarf measures approximately 60" (152.5 cm) from beginning ch **or** to desired length.

Finish off.

HAT
Ch 4; join with slip st to form a ring.

Rnd 1 (Right side)**:** Ch 1, 14 sc in ring; join with slip st to first sc.

Rnd 2: Ch 3 **(counts as first dc)**, dc in same st, 2 dc in next sc and in each sc around; join with slip st to first dc: 28 dc.

Rnd 3: Ch 1, **turn**; (sc, dc) in next dc and in each dc around; join with slip st to first sc: 56 sts.

Rnds 4-30: Ch 1, turn; (sc in next dc, dc in next sc) around; join with slip st to first sc.

Finish off.

Fold edge up for brim.

fisherman
HAT & SCARF SET

 ◼◼◻◻ **EASY**

Finished Sizes
Scarf: 6¼"w x 56"l (16 cm x 142 cm)
Hat: Fits 21" (53.5 cm) head circumference

MATERIALS
Medium Weight Yarn 【4】
[7 ounces, 364 yards
(198 grams, 333 meters) per skein]:
  2 skeins
Crochet hooks, sizes J (6 mm) **and** K (6.5 mm)
  or sizes needed for gauge
Yarn needle

GAUGE: With smaller size hook,
    12 sc and 12 rows = 4" (10 cm)

Gauge Swatch: 4" (10 cm) square
With smaller size hook, ch 13.
Row 1: Sc in second ch from hook and in each
ch across: 12 sc.
Rows 2-12: Ch 1, turn; sc in each sc across.
Finish off.

STITCH GUIDE
POPCORN (uses one st or sp)
4 Sc in st or sp indicated, drop loop from
hook, insert hook from **front** to **back** in first
sc of 4-sc group, hook dropped loop and
draw through st, ch 1 to close.
DECREASE
Pull up a loop in each of next 2 sc, YO and
draw through all 3 loops on hook **(counts as
one sc).**

SCARF
With smaller size hook, ch 170.

Row 1 (Right side)**:** Sc in second ch from hook
and in each ch across: 169 sc.

Note: Loop a short piece of yarn around any
stitch to mark Row 1 as **right** side.

Row 2: Ch 1, turn; sc in each sc across.

Row 3: Ch 1, turn; slip st in Front Loop Only of
each sc across **(Fig. 2, page 18)**.

Row 4: Ch 1, turn; working in free loops of sc
one row **below (Fig. 1a, page 18)**, sc in each sc
across.

Row 5: Ch 1, turn; working in both loops, sc in
first sc, [ch 3, skip next 2 sc, sc in next sc **(Fig. A)**,
turn; sc in each ch just made **(Fig. B)**, slip st in
next sc (sc before ch was begun) **(Fig. C), turn;**
working **behind** ch-3, sc in each of 2 skipped sc
(Fig. D) (first Cable made)], ★ ch 3, skip st where
previous ch was attached and next 2 sc, sc in
next sc, **turn;** sc in each ch just made, slip st in
next sc (sc before ch was begun), **turn;** working
behind ch-3, sc in each of 2 skipped sc (Cable
made); repeat from ★ across, sc in last sc (same
st where previous ch was attached): 56 Cables.

Fig. A

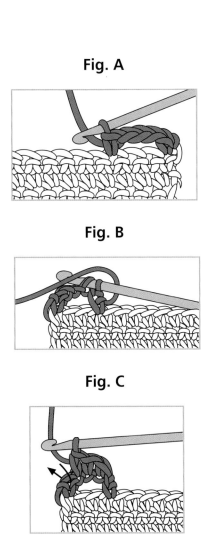

Fig. B

Fig. C

Fig. D

Row 6: Ch 1, turn; sc in first sc and in next 2 sc (behind first Cable), ★ skip sc where ch was attached on previous row, 2 sc in next sc (behind Cable), sc in next sc (behind same Cable); repeat from ★ across, sc in last sc (same st where previous ch was attached): 169 sc.

Instructions continued on page 12.

Row 7: Ch 1, turn; slip st in Front Loop Only of each sc across.

Row 8: Ch 1, turn; working in free loops of sc one row **below**, sc in each sc across.

Row 9: With larger size hook, ch 1, turn; working in both loops, sc in first sc, ★ ch 1, skip next sc, work Popcorn in next sc, ch 1, skip next sc, sc in next sc; repeat from ★ across: 43 sc, 42 Popcorns and 84 ch-1 sps.

Row 10: Ch 1, turn; sc in first sc and in next ch-1 sp, (ch 1, sc in next ch-1 sp) across to last sc, sc in last sc: 86 sc and 83 ch-1 sps.

Row 11: Ch 1, turn; sc in first sc, ch 1, sc in next ch-1 sp, ch 1, ★ work Popcorn in next ch-1 sp, ch 1, sc in next ch-1 sp, ch 1; repeat from ★ across to last 2 sc, skip next sc, sc in last sc: 44 sc, 41 Popcorns, and 84 ch-1 sps.

Row 12: Repeat Row 10.

Row 13: Ch 1, turn; sc in first sc, ch 1, work Popcorn in next ch-1 sp, ch 1, ★ sc in next ch-1 sp, ch 1, work Popcorn in next ch-1 sp, ch 1; repeat from ★ across to last 2 sc, skip next sc, sc in last sc: 43 sc, 42 Popcorns, and 84 ch-1 sps.

Rows 14 and 15: Repeat Rows 10 and 11.

Row 16: With smaller size hook, ch 1, turn; 2 sc in each ch-1 sp across, sc in last sc: 169 sc.

Rows 17-22: Repeat Rows 3-8.

Row 23: Ch 1, turn; sc in both loops of each sc across.

Edging Rnd: Ch 1, turn; slip st in each sc across, ch 1; work 11 sc evenly spaced across end of rows, ch 1; working in free loops of beginning ch **(Fig. 1b, page 18)**, slip st in each ch across, ch 1; work 11 sc evenly spaced across end of rows, ch 1; join with slip st to first slip st, finish off.

Holding 14 strands together, each 16" (40.5 cm) long, add fringe evenly spaced across sc on each end of Scarf **(Figs. 5a & b, page 19)**.

HAT
BODY

With smaller size hook, ch 26.

Row 1: Sc in second ch from hook and in each ch across: 25 sc.

Row 2 (Right side)**:** Ch 1, turn; slip st in Front Loop Only of each sc across.

Note: Mark Row 2 as **right** side.

Row 3: Ch 1, turn; working in free loops of sc one row **below**, sc in each sc across.

Row 4: Ch 1, turn; working in both loops, sc in first sc, [ch 3, skip next 2 sc, sc in next sc, **turn**; sc in each ch just made, slip st in next sc (sc before ch was begun), **turn**; working **behind** ch-3, sc in each of 2 skipped sc (first Cable made)], ★ ch 3, skip st where previous ch was attached and next 2 sc, sc in next sc, **turn**; sc in each ch just made, slip st in next sc (sc before ch was begun), **turn**; working **behind** ch-3, sc in each of 2 skipped sc (Cable made); repeat from ★ across, sc in last sc (same st where previous ch was attached): 8 Cables.

Row 5: Ch 1, turn; sc in first sc and in next 2 sc (behind first Cable), ★ skip sc where ch was attached on previous row, 2 sc in next sc (behind Cable), sc in next sc (behind same Cable); repeat from ★ across to last sc, sc in last sc: 25 sc.

Row 6: Ch 1, turn; slip st in Front Loop Only of each sc across.

Row 7: Ch 1, turn; working in free loops of sc one row **below**, sc in each sc across.

Row 8: With larger size hook, ch 1, turn; working in both loops, sc in first sc, ★ ch 1, skip next sc, work Popcorn in next sc, ch 1, skip next sc, sc in next sc; repeat from ★ across: 7 sc, 6 Popcorns, and 12 ch-1 sps.

Row 9: Ch 1, turn; sc in first sc and in next ch-1 sp, (ch 1, sc in next ch-1 sp) across to last sc, sc in last sc: 14 sc and 11 ch-1 sps.

Row 10: Ch 1, turn; sc in first sc, ch 1, sc in next ch-1 sp, ch 1, ★ work Popcorn in next ch-1 sp, ch 1, sc in next ch-1 sp, ch 1; repeat from ★ across to last 2 sc, skip next sc, sc in last sc: 8 sc, 5 Popcorns, and 12 ch-1 sps.

Row 11: Repeat Row 9.

Row 12: Ch 1, turn; sc in first sc, ch 1, work Popcorn in next ch-1 sp, ch 1, ★ sc in next ch-1 sp, ch 1, work Popcorn in next ch-1 sp, ch 1; repeat from ★ across to last 2 sc, skip next sc, sc in last sc: 7 sc, 6 Popcorns, and 12 ch-1 sps.

Rows 13 and 14: Repeat Rows 9 and 10.

Row 15: With smaller size hook, ch 1, turn; 2 sc in each ch-1 sp across, sc in last sc: 25 sc.

Rows 16-71: Repeat Rows 2-15, 4 times.

Joining Row: Ch 1, turn; with **right** side together, matching free loops of beginning ch with sc on Row 71, slip st in each st across working through **both** thicknesses; do **not** finish off.

CROWN

Rnd 1: Ch 1, turn; with **right** side facing and working in end of rows on Body, work 60 sc evenly spaced around; join with slip st to first sc.

Rnd 2: Ch 1, do **not** turn; beginning in same st as joining, decrease around; join with slip st to first sc: 30 sc.

Rnd 3: Ch 1, sc in each sc around; join with slip st to first sc.

Rnd 4: Ch 1, sc in same st, decrease, (sc in next sc, decrease) around; join with slip st to first sc: 20 sc.

Rnds 5 and 6: Ch 1, beginning in same st, decrease around; join with slip st to first sc; at end of Rnd 6, finish off leaving a long end for sewing: 5 sc.

Thread yarn needle with long end and weave through sts on Rnd 6; pull **tightly** to close and secure end.

BRIM

Foundation Rnd: With **right** side facing, using smaller size hook, and working in end of rows on Body, join yarn with slip st in any row; ch 1, work 60 sc evenly spaced around; join with slip st to first sc.

Row 1: Ch 10, sc in second ch from hook and in each ch across; slip st in next 2 sc on Foundation Rnd: 9 sc and 2 slip sts.

Row 2: Ch 1, turn; skip first 2 slip sts, sc in Back Loop Only of each sc across *(Fig. 2, page 18)*: 9 sc.

Row 3: Ch 1, turn; sc in Back Loop Only of each sc across; slip st in both loops of next 2 sc on Foundation Rnd: 9 sc and 2 slip sts.

Rows 4-58: Repeat Rows 2 and 3, 27 times; then repeat Row 2 once **more**.

Row 59: Ch 1, turn; sc in Back Loop Only of each sc across; slip st in **both** loops of next 2 sc on Foundation Rnd, slip st in same sc on Foundation Rnd (last slip st is worked in same st as Foundation Rnd joining).

Joining Row: Ch 1, turn; matching sc on Row 59 with free loops of beginning ch-10 and working through **both** thicknesses, slip st in Back Loop Only of sc **and** in free loop of beginning ch across; finish off.

Fold edge up for Brim.

braided
HAT & SCARF SET

 **EASY**

Finished Sizes
Scarf: 6"w x 58"l (15 cm x 147.5 cm)
Hat: Fits 21" (53.5 cm) head circumference

MATERIALS
 Medium Weight Yarn **4**
 [3.5 ounces, 170 yards
 (100 grams, 156 meters) per skein]:
 4 skeins
 Crochet hook, size J (6 mm) **or** size needed
 for gauge
 Yarn needle

GAUGE: 12 sc and 12 rows = 4" (10 cm)

Gauge Swatch: 6"w x 4"h (15 cm x 10 cm)
Work same as Scarf through Row 12.

STITCH GUIDE
POPCORN (uses one sc)
4 Sc in sc indicated, drop loop from hook,
insert hook from **front** to **back** in first sc of
4-sc group, hook dropped loop and draw
through st.
FRONT POST DOUBLE CROCHET
 (abbreviated FPdc)
YO, insert hook from **front** to **back** around
post of st indicated **(Fig. 3, page 19)**, YO and
pull up a loop (3 loops on hook), (YO and
draw through 2 loops on hook) twice.
BACK POST DOUBLE CROCHET
 (abbreviated BPdc)
YO, insert hook from **back** to **front** around
post of FPdc indicated **(Fig. 3, page 19)**, YO
and pull up a loop (3 loops on hook), (YO
and draw through 2 loops on hook) twice.
DECREASE
Pull up a loop in each of next 2 sc, YO and
draw through all 3 loops on hook **(counts as
one sc)**.

SCARF
Ch 19.

Row 1: Sc in second ch from hook and in each
ch across: 18 sc.

Row 2 (Right side): Ch 1, turn; sc in first 3 sc,
work Popcorn in next sc, sc in next 2 sc, work
FPdc around each of next 6 sc, sc in next 2 sc,
work Popcorn in next sc, sc in last 3 sc: 10 sc,
6 FPdc, and 2 Popcorns.

Note: Loop a short piece of yarn around any
stitch to mark Row 2 as **right** side.

Instructions continued on page 16.

Row 3: Ch 1, turn; sc in first 6 sts, skip next 2 FPdc, work BPdc around each of next 2 FPdc, working **behind** last 2 BPdc made, work BPdc around each of 2 skipped FPdc, work BPdc around each of next 2 FPdc, sc in last 6 sts: 12 sc and 6 BPdc.

Row 4: Ch 1, turn; sc in first 3 sc, work Popcorn in next sc, sc in next 2 sc, skip next 2 BPdc, work FPdc around each of next 2 BPdc, working in **front** of last 2 FPdc made, work FPdc around each of 2 skipped BPdc, work FPdc around each of next 2 BPdc, sc in next 2 sc, work Popcorn in next sc, sc in last 3 sc: 10 sc, 6 FPdc, and 2 Popcorns.

Repeat Rows 3 and 4 for pattern until Scarf measures approximately 58" (147.5 cm) from beginning ch **or** to desired length, ending by working Row 3.

Finish off.

HAT
Ch 68.

Row 1: Sc in second ch from hook and in each ch across: 67 sc.

Row 2 (Right side)**:** Ch 1, turn; sc in first 2 sc, work Popcorn in next sc, sc in next 2 sc, work FPdc around each of next 6 sc, ★ sc in next 2 sc, work Popcorn in next sc, sc in next 2 sc, work FPdc around each of next 6 sc; repeat from ★ across to last sc, sc in last sc: 25 sc, 36 FPdc, and 6 Popcorns.

Note: Mark Row 2 as **right** side.

Row 3: Ch 1, turn; sc in first sc, ★ skip next 2 FPdc, work BPdc around each of next 2 FPdc, working **behind** last 2 BPdc made, work BPdc around each of 2 skipped FPdc, work BPdc around each of next 2 FPdc, sc in next 5 sts; repeat from ★ across: 31 sc and 36 BPdc.

Row 4: Ch 1, turn; sc in first 2 sc, work Popcorn in next sc, sc in next 2 sc, skip next 2 BPdc, work FPdc around each of next 2 BPdc, working in **front** of last 2 FPdc made, work FPdc around each of 2 skipped BPdc, work FPdc around each of next 2 BPdc, ★ sc in next 2 sc, work Popcorn in next sc, sc in next 2 sc, skip next 2 BPdc, work FPdc around each of next 2 BPdc, working in **front** of last 2 FPdc made, work FPdc around each of 2 skipped BPdc, work FPdc around each of next 2 BPdc; repeat from ★ across to last sc, sc in last sc: 25 sc, 36 FPdc, and 6 Popcorns.

Rows 5-19: Repeat Rows 3 and 4, 7 times; then repeat Row 3 once **more**; at end of Row 19, do **not** turn; join with slip st to first sc on Row 19.

SHAPING
Rnd 1: Ch 1, turn; sc in same st as joining, ★ decrease, work Popcorn in next sc, decrease, skip next 2 BPdc, work FPdc around each of next 2 BPdc, working in **front** of last 2 FPdc made, work FPdc around each of 2 skipped BPdc, work FPdc around each of next 2 BPdc; repeat from ★ around; join with slip to first sc: 55 sts.

Rnd 2: Ch 1, do **not** turn; sc in same st, decrease around; join with slip st to first sc: 28 sc.

Rnd 3: Ch 1, sc in same st and in each sc around; join with slip st to first sc.

Rnd 4: Ch 1, sc in same st, (decrease, sc in next sc) around; join with slip st to first sc: 19 sc.

Rnd 5: Ch 1, sc in same st, decrease around; join with slip st to first sc: 10 sc.

Rnd 6: Ch 1, beginning in same st, decrease around; join with slip st to first sc, finish off leaving a long end for sewing: 5 sc.

Thread yarn needle with long end and weave through sts on Rnd 6; pull **tightly** to close. With **right** side together, sew back seam; secure end.

general INSTRUCTIONS

ABBREVIATIONS

BPdc	Back Post double crochet(s)
ch(s)	chain(s)
cm	centimeters
hdc	half double crochet(s)
dc	double crochet(s)
FPdc	Front Post double crochet(s)
mm	millimeters
Rnd(s)	Round(s)
sc	single crochet(s)
sp(s)	space(s)
st(s)	stitch(es)
tr	treble crochet(s)
YO	yarn over

★ — work instructions following ★ as many **more** times as indicated in addition to the first time.

( ) or [ ] — work enclosed instructions **as many** times as specified by the number immediately following **or** work enclosed instructions in the stitch or space indicated **or** contains explanatory remarks.

colon (:) — the number(s) given after a colon at the end of a row or round denote(s) the number of stitches or spaces you should have on that row or round.

■□□□ BEGINNER		Projects for first-time crocheters using basic stitches. Minimal shaping.
■■□□ EASY		Projects using yarn with basic stitches, repetitive stitch patterns, simple color changes, and simple shaping and finishing.
■■■□ INTERMEDIATE		Projects using a variety of techniques, such as basic lace patterns or color patterns, mid-level shaping and finishing.
■■■■ EXPERIENCED		Projects with intricate stitch patterns, techniques and dimension, such as non-repeating patterns, multi-color techniques, fine threads, small hooks, detailed shaping and refined finishing.

Yarn Weight Symbol & Names	LACE 0	SUPER FINE 1	FINE 2	LIGHT 3	MEDIUM 4	BULKY 5	SUPER BULKY 6
Type of Yarns in Category	Fingering, 10-count crochet thread	Sock, Fingering Baby	Sport, Baby	DK, Light Worsted	Worsted, Afghan, Aran	Chunky, Craft, Rug	Bulky, Roving
Crochet Gauge* Ranges in Single Crochet to 4" (10 cm)	32-42 double crochets**	21-32 sts	16-20 sts	12-17 sts	11-14 sts	8-11 sts	5-9 sts
Advised Hook Size Range	Steel*** 6,7,8 Regular hook B-1	B-1 to E-4	E-4 to 7	7 to I-9	I-9 to K-10.5	K-10.5 to M-13	M-13 and larger

*GUIDELINES ONLY: The chart above reflects the most commonly used gauges and hook sizes for specific yarn categories.

** Lace weight yarns are usually crocheted on larger-size hooks to create lacy openwork patterns. Accordingly, a gauge range is difficult to determine. Always follow the gauge stated in your pattern.

*** Steel crochet hooks are sized differently from regular hooks—the higher the number the smaller the hook, which is the reverse of regular hook sizing.

CROCHET HOOKS	
Metric mm	U.S.
2.25	B-1
2.75	C-2
3.25	D-3
3.5	E-4
3.75	F-5
4	G-6
5	H-8
5.5	I-9
6	J-10
6.5	K-10 1/2
9	N
10	P
15	Q

CROCHET TERMINOLOGY		
UNITED STATES		INTERNATIONAL
slip stitch (slip st)	=	single crochet (sc)
single crochet (sc)	=	double crochet (dc)
half double crochet (hdc)	=	half treble crochet (htr)
double crochet (dc)	=	treble crochet(tr)
treble crochet (tr)	=	double treble crochet (dtr)
double treble crochet (dtr)	=	triple treble crochet (ttr)
triple treble crochet (tr tr)	=	quadruple treble crochet (qtr)
skip	=	miss

GAUGE

Exact gauge is **essential** for proper fit. Before beginning your project, make the sample swatch given in the individual instructions in the yarn and hook specified. After completing the swatch, measure it, counting your stitches and rows/rounds carefully. If your swatch is larger or smaller than specified, **make another, changing hook size to get the correct gauge.** Keep trying until you find the size hook that will give you the specified gauge. Once proper gauge is obtained, measure width of piece approximately every 3" (7.5 cm) to be sure gauge remains consistent.

HINTS

As in all crocheted pieces, good finishing techniques make a big difference in the quality of the piece. Make a habit of taking care of loose ends as you work. Thread a yarn needle with the yarn end. With **wrong** side facing, weave the needle through several stitches, then reverse the direction and weave it back through several stitches. When ends are secure, clip them off close to work.

FREE LOOPS

After working in Back or Front Loops Only on a row or round, there will be a ridge of unused loops. These are called the free loops. Later, when instructed to work in the free loops of the same row or round, work in these loops **(Fig. 1a)**.

When instructed to work in free loops of a chain, work in loop indicated by arrow **(Fig. 1b)**.

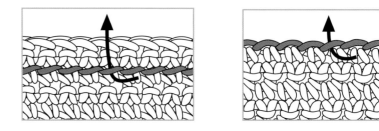

Fig. 1a   Fig. 1b

BACK OR FRONT LOOP ONLY

Work only in loop(s) indicated by arrow **(Fig. 2)**.

Fig. 2

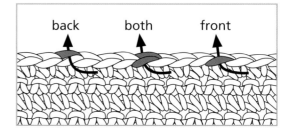

POST STITCH

Work around post of stitch indicated, inserting hook in direction of arrow *(Fig. 3)*.

Fig. 3

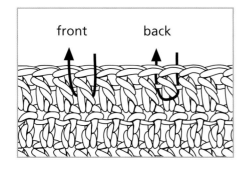

WORKING IN SPACE BEFORE A STITCH

When instructed to work in space **before** a stitch or in spaces **between** stitches, insert hook in space indicated by arrow *(Fig. 4)*.

Fig. 4

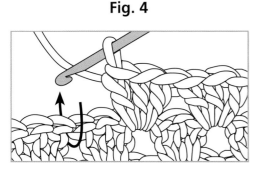

FRINGE

Cut a piece of cardboard 6" (15 cm) wide and 8" (20.5 cm) long. Wind the yarn **loosely** and **evenly** lengthwise around the cardboard until the card is filled, then cut across one end; repeat as needed. Hold together as many strands as specified in individual instructions; fold in half.

With **wrong** side facing and using a crochet hook, draw the folded end up through a stitch and pull the loose ends through the folded end *(Fig. 5a)*; draw the knot up tightly *(Fig. 5b)*. Repeat, spacing as specified in individual instructions.

Lay flat on a hard surface and trim the ends.

Fig. 5a

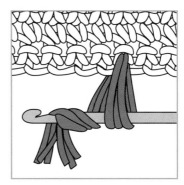

Fig. 5b

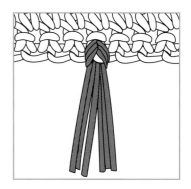

yarn
INFORMATION

Each Set in this leaflet was made using medium weight yarn. Any brand of medium weight yarn may be used. It is best to refer to the yardage/meters when determining how many balls or skeins to purchase. Remember, to arrive at the finished size, it is the GAUGE/TENSION that is important, not the brand of yarn.

For your convenience, listed below are the specific yarns used to create our photography models.

BASKET WEAVE HAT & SCARF SET
Lion Brand® Wool-Ease®
#140 Rose Heather

FISHERMAN HAT & SCARF SET
Red Heart® Super Saver®
#313 Aran

WOVEN STITCH HAT & SCARF SET
Bernat® Super Value
53044 True Grey

BRAIDED HAT & SCARF SET
Lion Brand® Vanna's Choice®
#108 Dusty Blue

TWO STITCH HAT & SCARF SET
TLC® Essentials™
#2919 Barn Red

We have made every effort to ensure that these instructions are accurate and complete. We cannot, however, be responsible for human error, typographical mistakes, or variations in individual work.

Pieces made and instructions tested by Janet Akins.

Production Team: Writer – Linda Daley; Contributing Editor – Lindsay Diane White; Editorial Writer - Susan McManus Johnson, Senior Graphic Artist - Lora Puls; Graphic Artists - Angela Ormsby Stark and Janie Marie Wright; Photo Stylist - Cora Brown; and Photographer - Jason Masters.

For digital downloads of Leisure Arts' best-selling designs, visit http://www.leisureartslibrary.com